✔ KU-686-733

CONTENTS

The 30 Minutes Series

The Kogan Page 30 Minutes Series has been devised to give your confidence a boost when faced with tackling a new skill or challenge for the first time.

So the next time you're thrown in at the deep end and want to bring your skills up to scratch or pep up your career prospects, turn to the *30 Minutes Series* for help!

Titles available are:

30 Minutes Before Your Job Interview
30 Minutes Before a Meeting
30 Minutes Before a Presentation
30 Minutes to Boost Your Communication Skills
30 Minutes to Succeed in Business Writing
30 Minutes to Master the Internet
30 Minutes to Make the Right Decision
30 Minutes to Prepare a Job Application
30 Minutes to Write a Business Plan
30 Minutes to Write a Marketing Plan
30 Minutes to Write a Report
30 Minutes to Write Sales Letters

Available from all good booksellers.
For further information on the series, please contact:

Kogan Page, 120 Pentonville Road, London N1 9JN
Tel: 0171 278 0433 Fax: 0171 837 6348

INTRODUCTION

You are looking for a new job – or your first job – and have studied the best places to find news of one:

- Situations vacant columns in newspapers, magazines and trade journals
- *Jobsearch* (in your reference library or on subscription)
- Careers offices and their notice boards, run by your local authority, college or university
- Careers fairs
- The Internet (for BBC opportunities)
- Notice boards in front of industrial and commercial buildings
- Jobcentres.

High street employment agencies will interview you if they think you have potential, then arrange an interview with an employer if there is a suitable job on their books. No fee is charged to the employee.

One of the best sources of new jobs is the grapevine otherwise known as word of mouth. If your friends, family and past employers know you are looking around, they can alert you to jobs which will never be advertised or to rumours of recruitment.

Headhunters are high level recruitment consultants who have been commissioned to fill specific posts, and *they* make the initial approach.

Writing a letter and sending a CV (curriculum vitae = personal history) enables you to put yourself across to a potential employer in the best light – you choose what to say and how to express yourself. This approach will, you hope, impress the recipient and result in an interview.

Telephone applications are also discussed here, and suggestions offered for making them.

A job hunt is a time-consuming business, but if you can spare thirty minutes to read this book, it will help you to save preparation time and concentrate on essentials.

Examples given are based on information provided by job seekers and interviewers, whose identities have been disguised. Helpful suggestions from Julie Kaiser and Dinah Langley were greatly appreciated.

1

ASSEMBLE YOUR PAPERWORK

Finding a new job can be a job in itself, but it can be speeded up by careful preparation.

The basis of all good job applications is to have a folder of written information about yourself – a dossier – on which you can draw. You may feel it is all in your mind already, but until you set it down, will possibly not realise what may be relevant to particular circumstances.

When you are on the phone to an employer, you could easily forget an important detail if questioned without an outline CV beside the telephone. It will include information you need to prepare a formal application.

Whatever form it takes – written or oral – a job application is designed to ensure you obtain an interview. It 'sells' you to the employer, so needs to be:

- easily read
- attractively presented

- persuasive
- informative
- concise.

Collect these items:

- Pad and pen for drafting, or boot up your computer.
- Good, plain A4 writing paper with matching white envelopes (DN, 110 × 220 mm)
- Certificates, diplomas, documentation on exams passed, honours gained, achievements, awards and courses taken.

Make a file in which to keep copies of the letters and forms you send out, and note on the letters the results of your applications.

- Did you get an interview?
- Why do you think you weren't offered the job?
- What will you change in your next interview as a result?

Keep the 'live' applications at the top, but still hold on to the others. If you need to prove that you have been looking for work, this file will be useful evidence for your claim to benefit.

2

OUTLINE YOUR RECORD OF ACHIEVEMENT

Are you at school? In that case, you will have a National Record of Achievement to take with you when you leave to show employers.

Anyone who is planning to make job applications might find a record of achievement useful as a basis for their CV. You can make it a more personal document than the school leaver's version, and keep it as a private record of achievements and aspirations. If you ask yourself questions *now*, about what you want from life and where your education and training are intended to lead you, you will be more prepared to cope with the more demanding application forms (Chapter 9).

What do you want to do in life?

You must have thought about this when you faced your

first public examinations. The lucky ones who already had a goal would have chosen their subjects with it in mind, and possibly made an action plan against which achievements could be measured.

If you don't know what you want to do and are still looking for a role, you need to consider where your present activities are leading you. You need to combine provision for your future with enjoyment of what you do.

Many application forms ask graduates such questions as:

- What are your career objectives?
- Why have you chosen mechanical engineering as a career?

They will expect a reasoned answer. If you have made an action plan, you can trace back the course you have followed and set down in compelling words what motivated you.

- What alternative careers are you considering?

This is another question asked of graduate applicants. Your plan for the future should include back-up possibilities in case your favourite scheme fails to mature. Have you explored related areas?

The format

A loose-leaf document allows you to expand the record over years. If you ever reach a point when you feel you are making no progress, or things are going badly, look back over your aims and achievements to remind yourself of past accomplishments. It will boost your morale.

A standard format is useful to start with – it gives information at a glance and provides source material for your CV. The first six headings below are included in the National Record of Achievement:

PERSONAL DETAILS

- Name
- Address
- Date of birth
- List of schools and colleges attended

SCHOOL ACHIEVEMENTS

QUALIFICATIONS AND CREDITS

OTHER ACHIEVEMENTS AND EXPERIENCE

- Work experience, leisure activities, skills gained

A PERSONAL STATEMENT

- Assessment of progress to date

EMPLOYMENT HISTORY

- All jobs listed.

Anyone starting their own record, after school or college, might include:

AWARDS

Scholarship, Duke of Edinburgh's Award, prizes, awards outside school and college.

INTERESTS AND ACTIVITIES

Mention the part you play in your leisure activities: active or passive. Keen swimmer (life-saving certificate), soccer player, pianist (grade 5), listening to music, seeing friends, going to the disco, member of police cadets, St John Ambulance, playing word games, acting.

SKILLS

Remember particularly the skills which will transfer to the workplace: IT use, driving, good telephone manner, fluent writer, ability to handle payments, organising. Don't forget the equipment you can use: personal computer, photo-copier, hand tools, lawn mower.

ACTION PLAN

Your career aim: to be a superb actress, save the rain-forests, play for Newcastle, become a chartered accountant, a first class salesman, a chartered engineer, see the world, fly a plane for BA.

Follow the plan by mapping out the route to achievement – the skills to be acquired, the exams passed, the training – with a timescale.

Your plan for your future will be influenced by ambition, whether you want to be:

- Rich
- Powerful
- Influential
- Somewhere else
- Caring for others
- A parent
- Famous.

Finding your role can take time – sometimes years – so the sooner it is thought about, the sooner your career can be directed towards its achievement.

3

PREPARE A CV

A curriculum vitae or résumé is your personal history as it relates to education, training and employment. It is a document which 'sells' you to a prospective employer: the market stall on which you lay out the goods you have on offer. You choose what goes on the stall and how it is arranged. The employer doesn't know you, so has to rely on the display. In the CV and its covering letter you have the opportunity to present yourself in the best possible light.

A CV is the basic document for making job applications. If you have kept a record of achievement (Chapter 2), the information you need to start your CV will be right there.

Start a CV as soon as you are ready to launch yourself on to the job market, and keep it up until you retire. As you gain experience, new skills and qualifications, update it. Then revise it when you apply for advertised posts so that, as near as possible, what you offer matches what the employer is looking for. Major items only are included at this stage, with less relevant material cleared away.

How employers use CVs

When a large number of applications are received, CVs are used to exclude candidates as well as to prepare an interview shortlist. Any that do not meet the advertised criteria are put aside.

If you submit a neatly prepared, easily read document *and* you match the job requirements, you are in with a chance. That chance is improved if the CV shows you have experience or outstanding achievements which lift you above the average.

The particular activity is not necessarily job related. Finding it hard to choose between equally admirable candidates, one employer selected the interviewee who had done something different – he had been on a mountaineering expedition while at university.

If there is a poor response to an advertisement, some less alluring CVs *may* receive consideration, but in general the employer will tend to re-advertise in the hope of a better crop next time.

What to include

Employers look for staff who will be:

- Dedicated
- Enthusiastic
- Efficient
- Effective
- Economical/Profitable.

Your CV needs to emphasise these qualities in yourself, as well as offering:

- Qualifications
- Experience

- Know-how
- Ability
- Acceptable personality
- Potential to grow the business/enterprise.

Show that you are a problem-solver, not a problem-maker. Indications that you have been involved with an industrial tribunal as winner or loser will not be reassuring.

Most areas of a CV give little scope for fine prose, but when listing employment history, activities and interests or 'additional information', you can use job-related action words such as: administered, attended, budgeted, controlled, handled, implemented, planned, produced, solved, trained, won. They sound more positive than repeating did, went to, worked out, ran, made, got, and so on.

Current salary should not be mentioned in the CV. If the advertisement specifically asks for the information, 'Please send your CV including details of your current remuneration', put this in your cover letter.

Job changers and career movers can damage their prospects by including it. If a lower salary is on offer, they may put themselves out of the running; if they are currently earning a much lower salary than the job will offer, they may be considered of doubtful value. Try to hold back the information until interview, when it can be discussed. Never look too keen to accept much less than you are currently earning – the desperation could show through and could raise doubts about you.

Marital status. It is unnecessary to mention this, or how many children you have, unless it relates to the job.

References

First jobbers should give academic references unless a

15

personal one is asked for: head of school, head of department, tutor, for example. Other applicants need only say: 'References will be supplied on request'.

All job applicants should gain referees' permission before giving their names in a CV or at interview. Academic references will probably have been discussed while you were at school or college. Let the referees know about applications that begin to look promising so they are ready to provide an appropriate reference when requested.

When you are asked to give *personal references*, adult friends of the family are probably best, especially if they have status. They will be asked their opinion of your personal qualities, such as:

■ honesty

■ punctuality

■ reliability

■ temperament

and how long they have known you.

Some employers regard them as being of doubtful value because they believe no one would choose a referee likely to describe them in less than glowing terms.

The employer will approach referees directly. Sometimes a printed form is sent, and an answer will be required for each entry, such as:

■ How long has X worked for you?

■ What position did he/she fill? What were the duties?

■ What was his/her standard of performance?

■ What was his attendance record?

A question sometimes put to past employers:

■ Would you, given the chance, employ X again?

Chronological CVs

Events are written under standard headings in a chronological CV in date order; any gaps show up, so every year is accounted for. Headings are in capitals or bold letters, on the left-hand side, as shown below. You will normally provide the information below the headings, or to the right. Suggestions for completion are offered where there may be a choice.

SURNAME

Your family name.

FORENAMES

Your given names. If your gender is not obvious from your name, add (M) or (F), denoting male or female.

ADDRESS

Include postcode.

TELEPHONE NO

Dialling code plus number.
If it has an answerphone, say so.

DATE OF BIRTH

Spell out, eg 10 July 1979.

AGE LAST BIRTHDAY

NATIONALITY

If you require a work permit to work legally in the UK, the employer needs to know, and is now legally responsible for checking. Say here if you already hold a full work permit.

EDUCATION

List secondary schools, colleges and universities in order, their addresses and dates attended.

QUALIFICATIONS

List the ones most important to the employer first (degree, trade or professional qualification). State the examination, subject, pass grade or class obtained or expected. Full training courses undertaken relevant to your application.

EMPLOYMENT HISTORY

The most recent or current job first. Give dates, employer, job title and main duties, your level of authority.

INTERESTS AND ACTIVITIES

Show the extent of your participation (spectator, player, organiser, on committee). Awards related to activities.

ADDITIONAL INFORMATION

A chance to include a well-constructed paragraph or so on relevant items not covered elsewhere, eg disability. In this case, emphasise that it does not affect your ability to work well.

Additional information can also be included in the cover letter.

Depending on your experience and the level of job targeted, the information will be of variable importance.

Emphases will change and some early life experience be deleted as the career progresses.

Functional CVs

A functional CV shows how you have developed and used your skills, rather than offering a chronological rundown of your work experience.

It avoids revealing periods of absence from the job market, though these may have to be disclosed at interview or on an application form. Never lie – it is a legitimate reason for dismissal if discovered after being appointed – but also don't hasten to reveal information which will harm your chances. Some factors are better saved for the covering letter.

Career changers who wish to show only the experience relevant to their current career will also find this formula of use. They can mention their earlier career in the cover letter if they wish.

Example. A training post with a large company is sought.

SURNAME	
FORENAMES	
ADDRESS	
TELEPHONE NO	
DATE OF BIRTH	
AGE LAST BIRTHDAY	
EMPLOYMENT HISTORY	
Prospect Improvements Ltd, personnel trainers	■ Training ■ Making presentations
Waterside College of Commerce, Bucks	■ Lecturing ■ Teaching business

| Eden Engineering Products (add address) | subjects to adults, including business start-ups; use of spreadsheets, sales and marketing in business start-ups |
| | ■ Practical experience of export procedures, handling Spanish correspondence. |

This CV ignores the fact that the writer has no degree or teaching qualification (none is needed to teach adults), although she is experienced in practical subjects, having started as a bilingual secretary in the export department. She now hopes to gain a highly remunerated post with a *Times* 1000 company. She will send some of her training programmes with her letter, and present herself well at interview.

This formula can also be used to advantage by older people with employment problems by leaving out all dates and mention of age. If an employer is looking for sound experience, maturity, patience and reliability, a loosely constructed CV might work. Applicants could be slightly more forthcoming in the covering letter. If they gain an interview, much will depend on their *apparent* age, so smart appearance is essential.

Laying out your CV

Employers who have many applications to deal with have no time to pick through messy or confused ones. They prefer CVs to be:

- Typed in black on A4 white paper (easier to read, clearer for photocopying)
- Well laid out with clear headings
- Concise (preferably two sides only).

If you have trouble getting it on two sheets, using one side of the paper only, it needs tailoring to fit.

You may have access to a CV computer program, eg Microsoft, which will lay it out for you.

The examples on pages 22–32 offer suggestions for:

- School and college leavers
- Graduates
- Job changers
- People returning to work after absence.

When you are satisfied with the result, check for: errors, omissions and spelling, or ask someone else to do so.

Take photocopies of the final version to send out. Keep the top copy.

No CV should be sent out except under cover of a letter. Examples of cover letters are given in Chapter 4.

Many recruitment agencies will prepare your CV, for a fee. However, you still need to produce the basic facts for them to work on. The result will be a beautiful document, more appropriate for a job changer or career mover than a beginner.

School leaver

Leslie has taken his GCSEs and is awaiting the results. He has a holiday job, and is expecting to do a BTEC in Business Studies next year. However, his father has health problems and money is a bit tight, and he feels this job is worth investigating. If he were successful, he could study in his own time to supplement the training given.

There will be great competition for the post. Few jobs are advertised for school leavers, and this offers a good starting salary (K = thousand) plus training (probably on computers). The sooner applications are submitted, the better.

ACCOUNTS CLERK

£8–£10K

Excellent opportunity for a school leaver educated to GCSE level. Working within a team of six, must be a quick learner; training given.

Send CV to David Craig, Clark Farrell Computing Ltd, Clark House, 2 Belvedere Road, London SW1G 2HL. (No agencies, phone calls or faxes.)

Students who have taken English, maths and computer studies would probably get preference, but a skill or aptitude test may be administered, especially if GCSE results are still awaited. The company wants to consider written applications and not be hassled by telephone calls.

Working in a team means being able to get on well with people; the rest of the team would probably meet short-listed applicants.

CURRICULUM VITAE

Surname	Morton
Forenames	Leslie (M)
Address	45 Abbey Green, London SE2 4KP
Telephone	0181 000 0000
Date of birth	4 April 1981

Age last birthday 16

Nationality British

Education

1992–1997 Spring Grove School
Church Street, London SE2

Exams taken

Results not yet received.

GCSE English language
IT and Business studies
Maths
Geography
French

Employment

1996–97 Braden News, morning paper round.

Summer 1997 Netprice Supermarkets, floor assistant in school holidays.

Interests and activities

Chess Keen player in school Chess Club.

Music Flute player; I enjoy concerts and listening to records.

Equipment I can use

Personal computer; photocopier.

References

Mr R A James, Head of Maths, Spring Grove School
Mrs P M Mathers, Head of Business Studies, Spring Grove School

School and college leavers are expected to be competent users of personal computers, but be sure to mention it anyway in your CV, cover letter, or both.

23

College leaver

Tony will be leaving college soon and does not know what he wants to do. He is quite interested in several subjects, but not enough to specialise, and is looking for a job which offers training. He lives at home and his parents maintain him, but emphasise the importance being self-sufficient; they are both self-employed. This is the advertisement he answers:

TRAINEE LASER PRINTER OPERATOR

Required for direct marketing company. Would suit well-presented college leaver with good general education and some knowledge of computers. Training will be given in laser printing, digital printing and print finishing. Shift work involved. Salary according to age and experience. Please apply in writing to: Paul Derry, DM House, 75 Brook Street, London W5 1DP.

He hadn't thought of printing, but the visual component appeals, as well as the idea of shift work – possibly being free while others are working. Tony prepares a short CV, and sends it with the letter on page 41.

CURRICULUM VITAE

SURNAME	Campbell
FORENAMES	Anthony Wayne
ADDRESS	103 Milton Road, Kenton, HE5 2RP
TELEPHONE	0181 000 0000 Answerphone
DATE OF BIRTH	10 June 1979
AGE LAST BIRTHDAY	18
NATIONALITY	British

EDUCATION

1990–1995	Robert Owen School, Langley Road, Kenton, HE5 4EX
1995–1997	Kenton Tertiary College, Preston Road, Kenton, HE3 3BR

QUALIFICATIONS

Intermediate GNVQ	Media and Communications
GCSE	English and Art, B grade; History, Spanish, Maths, C grade; Chemistry D grade

WORK EXPERIENCE

Work placement	GR Directory Publishers, Kenton 1996 Entering data on advertising sales; General office assistant.
Summer 1996	Woodlands Camp, Eastbourne Escorting and supervising children in summer camp.

INTERESTS AND ACTIVITIES

Photography	Setting up and taking pictures; one of my pictures has been used in local magazine.

Meeting friends at sports club. Playing games.

Tennis	Coached children at Woodlands
Table tennis	Camp

SKILLS

I can use a personal computer (basic programming, DOS and Word Perfect 6); ride a motor bike; develop black and white film.

REFERENCES

Mrs Wendy Beecham, Kenton Tertiary College, Preston Road, Kenton HE3 3BR

Mr Norman Finch, Woodlands Camp, Beachy Way, Eastbourne BN21 4US

Graduate

Gaby is a methodical and analytical person, ambitious to succeed in a career. She sees her future in a large organisation, but not one so bureaucratic that individuals have little chance to make an impact. She therefore rules out an application to work for the European Commission and decides to concentrate on an international business: banking. She applies to one of the big banks for admission as a graduate trainee. A CV is not required as applicants have to complete the bank's own application form, but she had drafted one in readiness.

CURRICULUM VITAE (Draft)

Surname	LAMONT
Forenames	Gabriel Anne
Address	47 Southport Road, Manchester M10 2BY (temporary)
Telephone	0161 000 0000
Date of birth	5 January 1976; 21 last birthday
Nationality	Dual British/French
Education	St Paul's School, Lancaster LA1 3ST 1987–94 Manchester University 1994–97

Qualifications	BA Hons Politics, Philosophy and Economics (results awaited; expected class 2.1)
	A levels: English, French A grades
	    Economics, Geography B grades
	GCSEs: English, French, Geography
	    A grades
	    Maths, Physics, Chemistry
	    B grades
	    History C grade

Employment (Vacation work)	1992 Office assistant, Myllet Mail Order, Lancaster 1993 Care assistant, Hay Bank Nursing Home, Lathom 1994 Farm work in Picardy (mother's family) 1995, 1996 Battlefield Tours, guiding in northern France.
Interests and activities	Cinema. Secretary of Cinema Club at University; member of NFT, London. Winter sports. Skiing in French Alps. Skating. Orienteering.
Skills	Bilingual English-French IT: basic programming, WordPerfect Car driver, clean licence Able to handle travel party, with tour manager Good organiser

In her application form, Gaby will emphasise the value of her vacation work in developing organising and managing skills, and dealing with other people in various situations, as well as taking responsibility. She will also point out that her combined English and French background gives her a broader view of national economic and financial matters.

Job changer

Sanjay sees this advertisement in his trade journal, and considers it is within his range. He can progress no further in his present firm and feels there is little left for him to learn in the job. Once he has a Diploma in Marketing he can aim higher, and this large company would look good on his CV. The exam is not until next month, but if he waits, he may miss the chance.

PRODUCT MANAGER

An excellent opportunity has arisen in one of the world's leading companies. You will be responsible for creating and implementing innovative marketing plans involving direct mail, publicity, in-store promotions and exhibitions.

Of graduate calibre you will have sound experience in marketing, particularly direct mail, possess excellent copy-writing and organisational skills and have an enthusiastic and creative approach.

An attractive remuneration and benefits package is offered. Please apply with full CV, quoting current salary, to: Alex Singarida, Business Track Information Services, 103–105 Palmers End, Reading RG1 4ME.

The company has offices or representatives around the world, but the UK office will deal mainly with European and Commonwealth sales, as the headquarters is in the USA. This is not stated, but the company is well known, and Sanjay keeps up with trade news.

'Of graduate calibre' does not specify a degree, but marketing entrants are mainly graduates.

Direct mail will obviously be a major component of the job. Creativity and writing ability are vital for success, and the employer will probably ask short-listed candidates to submit a budgeted plan of compaign for a specific product to test their abilities.

Sanjay's previous experience has prepared him for this, but this organisation is in a bigger league, and the stakes will be higher. He is conversant with EU members' regulations on direct marketing, and is gaining knowledge about the rest of Europe.

By asking the current salary, the employer will be able to judge the applicants' expectations of the remuneration package, and adjust the proposed offer if necessary.

See his covering letter on page 42.

CURRICULUM VITAE

Surname	CHOPRA
Forenames	Sanjay (M)
Address	193 Highfield Road, Birmingham B3 B4X
Telephone	0121 000 0000
Date of birth	7 October 1970 (27 last birthday)
Nationality	British
Education	Sefton School, Moreton B8 7UP 1982–88 Hudson College, University of London 1989–92
Qualifications	BA Hons English with Business Studies A levels: English, German (A); Maths, Geography (B). Same subjects in GCSE plus IT, History and Art. Due to take Diploma in Marketing exam in June.
Employment history	1995–97 World Wide Directories Ltd, marketing executive

---

	responsible for raising uptake of software, CD-ROMs and book-form directories among business buyers. Planning and organising mailing programmes; analysing results. 1993–95 *The Executive Week*, marketing executive 1992–93 *The Daily Dealer*, space selling at first, followed by six months PR and promotions
Skills	Bilingual English-Hindi; competent user of Apple Mac; Excell; Word for Windows 6; Corel Draw; Paintbrush; clean driving licence; persuasive telephone manner; good organiser
Interests and activities	Writing for pleasure; puzzles and games – solving and setting; keen tennis player. Family.
Additional information	My interest in games arose from a request by my brother to help with devising interesting ways to teach children in a remedial class at his school. The exercises proved very useful and are to be published by IQ Press next year. I was able to build on this experience when devising mailing pieces. My interest in design enables me to support and enhance the copy through visual means.

Returners to work

1. Woman returner whose children are now at school

Margaret sees this advertisement in her local newspaper. She has stayed at home since her children were born, but has been planning a return to work.

RECEPTIONIST/CASHIER

We need a new member of the team to help maintain our high standards of professional, client-focused service. The responsible role will involve you greeting and attending to patients as they arrive, handling payments and acting as first point of contact on the telephone. A well-spoken professional telephone voice, together with the ability to deal with patients on a one-to-one basis in a mature and pleasant manner is essential. Please send your CV to The Personnel Manager at City Laboratories Ltd, Health Care House, Jenner Street, Manchester M1 3UP.

No qualifications are mentioned, but the word 'professional' occurs twice, emphasising the image of this medical laboratory. They are looking for someone with an excellent telephone manner, a caring attitude towards patients and the ability to handle money. No age is given, but the advertisement implies that the post is not for youthful applicants.

Margaret's CV is comparatively short, and she can make a few points in the covering letter (see page 44).

CURRICULUM VITAE

Surname	Ferris
Forenames	Margaret Caroline
Address	103 Craven Road, Manchester M4 0TH
Telephone	0161 000 0000
Date of birth	14 March 1963; 34 last birthday
Nationality	British
Education	Selwyn School for Girls 1974–1979 Crofton College of Commerce 1979–1980
Qualifications	1980 Shorthand 120 wpm Typewriting 70 wpm Office Skills RSA O levels in English, Maths, French, History, Geography, Biology
Employment	1983–1986 Secretary to Personnel Director, Morton Assurance HQ 1980–83 Departmental secretary, Department of Education, Morton University

Other information

I was a very competent office worker when in full-time employment, but have since been bringing up my children. In the mean time, I have done voluntary work and handled our domestic budget.

4

WRITE A COVER LETTER

The letter which encloses your CV or application form gives you the chance to highlight your strengths or mention any factor which might affect your employment chances.

Presentation

This letter is a marketing tool which aims to 'sell' you to the employer. It needs to look clean and crisp and be easily read, to convey the impression that you work to these same standards.

A handwritten letter should be sent if an advertisement stipulates this; if no preference is stated, you can choose whether to write or type.

White A4 paper to match that used for your CV is best. Otherwise, any good, plain paper will be acceptable, provided it is not highly coloured. Blue or black ink is preferred.

Address the letter to the person named in the advertisement, in which case you sign off 'Yours sincerely'. If no name is given, and they simply say: 'Apply to the Personnel Department', start 'Dear Sirs' and sign off 'Yours faithfully'.

A specimen layout is given below. If you expect to move shortly, say so, and give the new address, if known, as well as the date of your move:

> 'I am at this address until the end of the month, but will be moving to — on the 31st, and the telephone number will be —.'

Ensure that the recipient knows where to make contact with you during working hours. If you have no fixed address, it is important to establish a place where messages will be taken and mail held for you to collect. Call in daily to be sure you miss nothing.

Specimen layout

Your address

Postcode

Your telephone no

Date in full, eg
7 July 1997

Addressee's name
(as it appears in the advertisement)

Address

Dear Mr/Mrs/Miss/Ms Name
(as it appears in the advertisement)

Introductory paragraph: mention advertisement, job and enclosure (CV *or* application form, not both).

What you can offer.

Explain personal circumstances (if applicable).

Last paragraph. If the advertisement asks you to give your current salary, do so here. Do not mention it otherwise.

Yours sincerely

Your signature

Your name spelled out

The text

Some examples are given in the following pages, but a few general points apply. It is inadvisable to criticise your present employer directly if you are asked to state a reason for wishing to leave. Show instead that you have outgrown the job or *you* may be thought difficult to work with.

You may be overworked, underpaid and stressed in your present job, but mention of it is best avoided when applying for a new one. They don't know you or your capacity for hard work, and may write you off as someone looking for an easy berth.

Examples

The short, sharp single paragraph

Dear Mr Carlisle

I have seen your advertisement in the *Gloucester Gazette* of 20 April and wish to apply for the post of Reservation Sales Agent. As you will see from my enclosed CV, I am well qualified in this area, and have had two years' experience with Marine Motels. I would welcome the chance to work for an international hotel group, and hope to be granted an interview. I look forward to hearing from you.

Yours sincerely

Always refer to the specific advertisement as well as the post applied for. Some companies will have several advertisements running at the same time, for different jobs, so state exactly what you are after.

Further to our telephone conversation when I requested details of the Reservation Sales Agent vacancy advertised in the *Gloucester Gazette* of 20 April, I now have pleasure in returning my completed application form.

'Marketing' paragraph

My GCSE results are not in yet, but I expect to do well, especially in English, maths and German, the subjects most relevant to the post advertised in your shipping office.

I have been in my present job nearly two years during which time I have been promoted from clerical duties to checking credit ratings and am now responsible for checking daily receipts against our business debtors list as well. I report to the credit controller, but the sales ledger department works as a harmonious team; I can offer the dedication and enthusiasm required in the new post, and get on well with colleagues.

> During my time at Peterborough Productions I have made considerable saving for the company, including rescheduling the sales periods from calendar months to four/five week periods, ending on Fridays; this allowed end-of-month reconciliation to be carried out on Saturdays, freeing up the computer system for the rest of the company during the five-day week. I moved much routine accounts work out of town to the warehouse area where hourly rates were lower. I am sure my experience in cost cutting would be of great value to your company.

Explanatory paragraph

This is where you comment on your personal circumstances, or paper over any cracks in your working history with information you prefer to omit from your CV.

Reasons for leaving your job could include:

- I feel I have the capacity to achieve more than I am able to do at present (your present job is boring).

- I am looking for a job in an expanding company which seems to offer greater chances of promotion and advancement (I am stuck in a rut; there are rumours of downsizing and I want to get a job that will last).

- I have reached the top of my grade and am ready to move on as soon as I get my diploma (there is no scope for promotion and I am underpaid).

- Our entire department was made redundant in April last year when the company cut back, and I have since been engaged in a variety of temporary jobs, mainly through Willpower Agency, who will vouch for me. It would be very satisfying to use my skills and have the opportunity to show commitment on a longer-term basis.

In this explanatory paragraph, women returners could allay any worries about who will care for their children when they are ill or on holiday.

A disabled person would emphasise that their minor disability has no effect on their work other than to motivate them to try harder. Stress what you can do well.

Job-share applicants will need to show how they will cover the job between them and put a hand-over routine in place.

Anyone leaving the armed services for civilian life should avoid service jargon – which the employer may not understand – and 'translate' their experience into business or industrial terms.

It is important not to lie in any job application, as its discovery can result in dismissal once you are employed. Convictions which are not spent under the 1974 Rehabilitation of Offenders Act should not be concealed, but mentioned in the letter rather than the CV. If the cause has no bearing on the job, a lenient view might be taken, but a background of dangerous or drink driving will not persuade an employer to take you on as an area rep.

I do realise that this housing estate has an unfortunate reputation, but this is down to a small group whose activities get written up in the papers. We are mainly law-abiding and hard-working, and I hope to be given the chance to prove this to an employer.

My circumstances require some explanation. I was a very successful sales representative for Steel Valves Inc, but lost my job through a driving incident. I am not yet back on the road, but feel that my knowledge of the water supply industry could benefit your company immensely from a sales perspective. I would welcome the opportunity to put this to the test.

You say in your advertisement that a graduate is required; I consider myself to be educated to degree level. Family circumstances forced me to leave full-time education after A levels, and I have gained a Diploma in Animal Nutrition through part-time study since.

Closing paragraph(s)

A chance to say something complimentary about the company before signing off. This is also where you mention salary if the advertisement requires you to divulge it.

I look forward to hearing from you, and could be available for interview at any time except the week of 9 June, when I have examinations. I would very much like to work in a laboratory with such an excellent reputation for research.

I would be glad to supply any further information required, and hope to hear from you soon. I am available for interview now.

My current salary is £x, boosted by free staff canteen for lunch and interest-free season ticket loans. I would hope to match this, but could allow for a saving in fares by travelling less far. I look forward to hearing from you; I am keen to work for a leading manufacturer in the trade.

The hint about saving on fares is a way of indicating you could be flexible if they made you an offer.

At present I am earning £x, plus 2½ per cent commission on paid-up sales invoices; there is an adjustable bonus for on-target earnings. A company car and medical insurance are also part of the package. I would expect to do as well for your company as I do in my current job and would be willing to show commission statements at interview as proof of ability.

I look forward to hearing from you.

Some advertisers are very specific about what they want to have from applicants:

Applicants are invited to submit a CV and the names of two referees together with a letter explaining why you are interested in the appointment and how you meet its requirements.

Applications to be sent to — by Friday 25 April.

The following letters were sent by applicants whose CV appear in Chapter 3.

School leaver

Leslie is responding to the advertisement on page 22.

Dear Mr Craig

Accounts Clerk vacancy

I wish to be considered for the post of Accounts Clerk advertised in the Tribune dated 16 July. My CV is enclosed, and I could come for interview at any time.

I am keen to make a career working with figures.

Although my GCSE results have not come through yet, I expect to do well in maths, IT and business studies, and had intended to take a BTEC course next year. But when I saw your advertisement, I felt it was just what I wanted and I would leave school if you offered me the job. I could learn in my own time and on the job.

I am sure I have the enthusiasm and abilities you are looking for and hope to hear from you soon.

Yours sincerely

Leslie has written his application on the spur of the moment, so has not consulted his referees. If he gets an interview, he will need to write or phone them to explain the situation.

College leaver

Tony is applying for the post advertised on page 24.

Dear Mr Derry

I am very interested in your advertisement for a Trainee Laser Printer Operator in this week's *Middlesex Mail* and would like to apply.

I leave college this term, and have gained an Intermediate GNVQ in Media and Communications, as well as the GCSEs set out in my enclosed CV. As photography is one of my special interests, you can imagine that visual presentation is very important to me, and I am very keen to extend my knowledge of the processes of commercial production.

41

30 Minutes to Prepare a Job Application

> The lead tutor on the GNVQ course, Mrs Beecham, has offered to give me a reference; she has supervised us over the past year and knows our work well. I could come for interview right away, and hope to hear from you soon.
>
> Yours sincerely

The advertisement brought it home to Tony that he really would like to work in print; even if he is not successful this time, he now has a focus for his future job search.

Job changer

Sanjay is responding to the advertisement on page 28. Some marketing people fax a letter ahead of their CV but Sanjay realises that such a fanfare approach would be inappropriate for the advertiser and its businesslike image. He writes:

> Dear Mr Singarida
>
> ### PRODUCT MANAGER
>
> I wish to apply for this interesting post, advertised in the *Marketing Mouthpiece* of 18 May.
>
> I would welcome the opportunity to exploit, in a new business environment, the extensive experience I have gained in promoting business information media to executives, trainers and lecturers in higher education throughout Europe, the Far East and the Commonwealth.
>
> Most recently, I have run the launches of Factpool and Planmaster packages, as well as constantly improving

42

and monitoring the ongoing direct mail programme directed to our financial and management markets, extending appreciably our coverage in India and the Pacific Rim.

During my time at World Wide Directories I have created, budgeted, planned and executed several campaigns which have produced highly favourable results. A selection of the relevant mailing pieces is enclosed. In-store promotion plans are scheduled for a year ahead, and I have coordinated these with our Sales Department personnel.

I shall be sitting the CIM Diploma in Marketing exam next month, and could attend an interview most weeks but not between the 2nd and 6th June.

My current remuneration is £20,000 pa, plus medical insurance for myself and my family. I realise that relocation is likely to be involved, but do not see this as a problem. I would welcome the chance to work for your highly regarded company.

I look forward to hearing from you soon.

Yours sincerely

His CV is on page 29. He is excited at the possibility of a move; working in an international organisation would broaden his experience both in marketing and administration.

Returners to work

Margaret is responding to the advertisement on page 31.

Dear Sir

I am applying for the post of Receptionist/Cashier advertised in today's *Courier*, and my CV is enclosed. As you will see, my work has been mainly at home for some years now, looking after my two children, who are both at school.

During that time I have helped to run a local play group and later became membership secretary of our community association. Both voluntary positions required me to deal sympathetically with children and adults, as well as handling money. It meant also that my office skills were maintained.

I feel that my background and experience would fit me admirably for the post; I am keen to return to paid employment, and have arranged for my sister to care for the children once this is in place.

Hoping to hear from you soon, I am

Yours faithfully

See her CV on page 32. This would be her first job after eleven years away from the employment market and it offers an opportunity to use the skills she has developed at home. There will be no useful employment references available. The employer will probably phone to check her voice and telephone manner before offering an interview. Her appearance and manner will be important, as she will be the first person visitors see on arrival.

Replying to box numbers

Occasionally you will see an advertisement which gives no employer's name or address, only a box number. They usually appear in trade journals so as to target the right people, and replies are sent to the box number, c/o the publication.

No clues will be given to enable you to check out the particular company beyond its city of location – it may even be your own company!

Send a concise, factual letter and a CV tailored to the job if you are keen.

Writing the letter

Study the advertisement and your CV and:

- Make a draft, emphasising your suitability for the post, using positive and active expressions.
- Check the draft for correct spelling and grammar, or ask someone else to do so if you are unsure.
- Write or type a fair copy of the letter.
- Make a copy to keep. You may need it for reference and to take to the interview.
- Address the envelope, preferably one which involves folding the letter and enclosures no more than twice.
- Send the letter first class, but do not put it through your company's franking machine; some employers look out for applicants who they consider misuse their firm's facilities!

Be sure to post it so it arrives before the closing date for applications, if one has been given.

5

WRITE IN RESPONSE TO AN ADVERTISEMENT

Some advertisements will invite you to write for further details and an application form. A simple letter will suffice:

> Your address
>
> Postcode
>
> Your telephone no
>
> Date in full

Addressee's name (take it from the advertisement)

Address

Dear Mr/Mrs/Miss/Ms (take it from the advertisement)

Clinical Scientists

I have seen your advertisement in the current edition of the *New Scientist*, and should like to have full details, as

> well as an application form. I expect to graduate this year in Clinical Immunology and am most interested in the opportunity offered.
>
> Yours sincerely

Most advertisements ask for a CV, but sometimes they will say 'Apply in writing to: —'. It is usual to send a CV with a covering letter, but you may wish to write a letter which includes an outline CV. If you do this, be sure not to run over two pages.

The letter should be written afresh for each application and tailored to the individual advertisement. The presentation set out in Chapter 4 applies. If a reference is given, quote it.

Example

Read the advertisement carefully and list the requirements of the job. They are underlined here.

> We urgently require a <u>flexible and energetic administrator</u> to provide general support to a very busy sector. You will need to have a minimum of <u>five GCSEs or equivalent</u>, including <u>English language</u>. You must be fully conversant with <u>Paradox, Lotus 1 2 3 and WP6.1</u>, possess <u>good organisational skills</u> and have a <u>good telephone manner</u>.
>
> Please apply in writing to: —.

The qualifications and skills required are fairly cut and dried, so there is little point in applying if you do not possess them. No age is mentioned, so that area is open.

Neither is any remuneration package, so it will probably be scaled to the successful applicant.

Dear —

I am replying to your advertisement for an administrator which appeared in the *Glasgow Post* on 3 March.

I am sure I have the skills and experience you are looking for, having been office supervisor with Craig Health Trust for the past two years. There I was responsible for the smooth running of the office services, which included: the engagement of secretarial staff; the appointments system; handling consultants' mail (they dictated on audiotapes); filing; departmental accounts. We used the computer programs you mention: Paradox, Lotus 1 2 3 and WP6.1. I can also use Excell. I am used to working under pressure, and enjoyed good working relations with my own team and the medical staff.

Previously, I was a secretary at Third Age Retirement Homes, my first job after leaving secreterial college, where I worked from June 1973–April 1975. I travelled in Europe for three months, then did temporary work before joining Craig HT.

Education and training
Priory House Secretarial College 1973
Secretarial course comprising: audio typing, word processing, office skills to RSA III.

Denby Grammar School for Girls 1966–1972
HCE: English, History and Geography (grade B)
SCE: English, History, Geography, French, Chemistry, Physics and Maths.

Referee
Mr Neil Herd at Craig Health Trust. He knows I need to leave owing to my husband's company moving.

I look forward to hearing from you, and shall be happy to provide any further information or documentation you may require.

Yours faithfully

You may prefer to set your letter out like a CV: the choice is yours.

6

WRITE AN ON-SPEC LETTER

Speculative letters are sent to organisations that have not advertised a vacancy in the hope that they may have a job for you.

Many vacancies are never advertised; employers first consider an internal appointment or promotion then put the word round that they are looking for someone, saving on recruitment costs. Advertised vacancies represent the jobs for which this approach is inappropriate or ineffective: they are the tip of the iceberg.

Why approach a specific company?

- You may have been tipped off.

- You may have read about their expansion plans in the press, or heard news of their winning a big new contract.

- You may like what you have heard about the firm, or admire their products, and want to work for them.

Presentation

The letter needs to be well laid out (see Chapter 4), correctly spelled and punctuated. It must be written, typed or run off afresh for each addressee, and signed by you. Never send out photocopies (except for the enclosures); they look as though you have taken little trouble, and can inspire the reaction, 'If he's sent out dozens of these, I shan't bother with it.'

Enclosing a stamped-addressed envelope (SAE) should guarantee a response, but don't rely on it.

Address your letter to a named person; phone first to find out who to write to.

Enclosures

These can be photocopies. If you hold written references, keep the originals, and only ever send out photocopies.

If you are a school leaver, you can incorporate your CV in the letter, though this makes for a lot of copying when sending out several letters. Applicants with more experience should always send a CV.

Keep a log

Make a note of the firms you have written to, so you are prepared for a response at any time, perhaps months later.

Some firms will write back saying they have no vacancies at present, but will bear your name in mind when a suitable vacancy arises. Some of them even mean it!

Examples

Remember to offer them something: expertise, enthusiasm or willingness to learn.

Dear Mr Blake

I am writing at the suggestion of Roger Barnett to ask if you have any vacancies for production controllers on plant installation. We were colleagues at Servo Systems and he knows my work well. I have just completed my contract on the waste-processing installation in Merivale.

I see from the trade press that you are to build a new plant in Cumberland and thought you would be looking for people with the right expertise. My CV is enclosed.

I would welcome the chance to discuss possibilities with you.

Yours sincerely

Dear Mrs Porter

I am leaving school at the end of June and wonder whether you have a vacancy in Revvo Productions for a willing learner. I am waiting for my GCSE results in English, Maths, Chemistry, History and Geography, and can show you good annual reports. I can use a personal computer.

My only work experience has been helping in a hairdressing salon on Saturdays; I carried out specified tasks and made myself generally useful. The manager would give me a reference, if asked.

I am good with my hands, and would welcome the chance to find out if there is a suitable opening.

Yours sincerely

7

PHONE IN RESPONSE TO AN ADVERTISEMENT

You have seen a brilliant job advertisement and can't wait to phone the advertiser. Hold on a minute!

Pull out your CV first and underline in pencil the items particularly relevant to the job, emphasising the attributes, knowledge and experience required. This way you are less likely to overlook an important match between the employer's needs and what you have to offer.

In case an appointment is offered, have by you:

- Diary
- Pen and pencil for notes.

Be prepared to give your name and address, and a telephone number where you can be reached during business hours. Then call the number.

Why employers may prefer telephone calls

A telephone response:

- gives the employer an opportunity to check your speaking voice and telephone manner
- is a quicker and cheaper way of dealing with applications than opening up written submissions
- avoids initial judgements based on appearance at interview.

A heavy response enables the employer to apply a cut-off time for accepting calls about the job, so if you are looking in daily or local evening papers, it is important to do so as soon as they are on the streets. Vacancies in the London *Evening Standard* sometimes have a full list by lunch time. It is always worth trying later, but the really keen types will be ahead of you. Trade journals mostly require written applications.

Answering machines

The increased use of recorded message answering services in large organisations can be disconcerting. The voice will invite you to listen to a 'menu' of departments, asking you to press a specified button on your push-button phone when you hear the option you want.

- Listen carefully to the menu
- If the Personnel Department or the named person is not on the list, keep holding until you have a live-voice operator on the line, who will deal with your call.

This all costs money, so be sure you have spare cash or a reasonably new card if you are talking from a pay phone.

The telephone interview

Ask the operator for the person or department nominated in the advertisement:

> 'May I speak to Andrew East.'
> 'Putting you through.' Or: 'May I know what it is in connection with?'
> 'I'm responding to his advertisement in today's *Tribune*.'

Operators often need to ask the reason for your call, so they can pass it on when they announce you.

> 'Good morning. My name is George Tennyson. I am very interested in your advertisement for cabin crew in today's *Tribune*, and would like to apply.'

George sounds enthusiastic – as indeed he is – and is smiling. Even though no one can see him, he knows that if he smiles, he comes across as a friendly and positive person. He is always polite.

The advertisement that aroused his interest listed the following requirements for cabin crew at London airports.

- Ability to converse in any of 21 listed languages, any Scandinavian or East European language; and/or
- Certificated holders of sign language
- Ability to communicate confidently in different languages
- Right to live and work in the UK indefinitely
- Age 20 to 49
- Height 5'2" to 6'2" (1.57 to 1.88 m) with weight in proportion
- Fully conversant with the needs of customer service.

Applicants were to telephone Monday–Friday, 9am–6pm. A blend of linguistic and personal skills was called for, as well as the ability to form part of a successful team. As weekly office hours are given, applicants can prepare themselves and need not rush to the phone immediately.

The interviewer is filling in a form at his end, and says:

'Would you give me your name, address and daytime telephone number, please.'

'Date of birth?'

'Nationality?'

'Which language can you offer?'

'What experience have you had of dealing with the public?'

'Do you have any health problems? Are you fit?'

'When did you last visit your doctor?'

'How tall are you?' What do you weigh?'

'What are you doing now?'

Contact with the public could take many forms – it is the one requirement of the job which is not tightly prescribed.

Attributes such as

- Level-headedness
- Neat and well-groomed appearance
- Air of confidence and competence
- Dexterity

would be assessed at interview. Candidates would complete an application form, and if successful, undergo aptitude and attitude tests, as well as a rigorous training course before being let loose on passengers.

The terms and conditions would have been outlined briefly on the telephone, and spelled out in more detail at interview, but if you have questions which would affect your application, ask them while on the telephone.

8

PHONE ON SPEC – COLD CANVASSING

Speculative telephone calls are made for the same reason as speculative letters are sent, but the response is quicker, and you obviously feel confident of your telephone manner.

Telephone calls are interactive and – unless you are well prepared or have the relevant documents in front of you – unexpected questions could put you off your stride, so have to hand:

- CV
- Pad and pencil
- Diary.

Speak to the switchboard operator and ask for the name of the manager in charge of recruitment or, if there is one, the personnel manager. Ask to be put through.

'May I ask what the call is in connection with?'
'Motor car sales. I'm used to demonstrating new models

for clients, and wondered whether you had any vacancies.'
'One moment, please...We have nothing at present, I'm
afraid; we usually advertise our vacancies in the
Courier.'

Keep trying.

'Could I speak to your managing editor, please? What is
the name?'
'One moment, please.'
'Joanna Crane speaking.'
'I'm James Grainger, and have been an editor with
Zircon; they are now cutting back and I wondered if you
had any vacancies or freelance opportunities.'
'What was your subject area? Were you desk editing or
commissioning or both?'
'I'm a specialist in politics and history.'
'We might just have something. Would you care to send
me your CV and we'll be in touch.'

It may be that you were recommended to make contact by
someone with inside information. Check with that person
before you mention their name to the company you call, if
they haven't authorised you to do so.

9

FILL IN THE APPLICATION FORM

Some employers will ask you to complete an application form. Although they may already have your CV, they want the information from all applicants presented in a standard format which makes for easier comparison. Your CV provides you with much of the information, although it may need rejigging to fit the formula, so you see the value of having a CV ready at all times. Never write in a box 'See CV' – always rewrite the information to fit.

Make a draft

If you can, photocopy the form, but in any case draft your answers before attempting to write on the master. Where space allows, use complete sentences and lose no opportunity to put your merits and achievements across.

You should read the instructions with care. They mean it when they ask for block capitals, black or blue ink. Some will specify typescript or handwriting. For one thing, when the document is photocopied, they want good, legible writing. For another, it is a check on how carefully you read and carry out simple instructions for completing and posting the documents.

A draft will help to ensure that your answers fit the space provided and that no vital information is omitted. It can be difficult to fit typescript into small boxes. Generally speaking, if a small box is given, a short answer is likely to be required. If you must add more, attach an extra sheet of paper headed with your name, but remember that your application is probably one of many and excessive length will tell against you.

Specimen headings

Headings from a selection of employers' forms are given below, with notes on their completion. Students applying from university may be using the AGCAS Standard Application Form (or SAF) which they will head with the name of the employer, whose instructions will have been provided separately.

EMPLOYER'S NAME

POSITION APPLIED FOR

SURNAME (Mr, Mrs, Miss, Ms)

FORENAMES

PREVIOUS NAME (if applicable)

PRESENT ADDRESS
　　　　　　　　Include postcode.

TELEPHONE NO
　　　　　　　　Say if it is an answerphone or
　　　　　　　　fax; give dialling code and
　　　　　　　　number.

PERMANENT ADDRESS
(if present address See above.
is temporary)

TELEPHONE NO

DATE OF BIRTH
      Spell out, eg 7 April 1974.

AGE LAST BIRTHDAY

PLACE OF BIRTH

NATIONALITY

If you require a work permit to work legally in the UK, the employer needs to know, and is now legally responsible for checking. Say here if you already hold a full work permit.

EDUCATION (in order of importance to employer)

University	Dates	Degree and Department Title and class PhD: Supervisor's name 'Results not yet known' will suffice if you are awaiting them.
College	Dates	Exams passed (date and grade)
Secondary School	Dates	Exams passed (date and grade)
Other courses		Omit short courses, but include others relevant to the job applied for.

AWARDS

Arising from interests or work. Blow your trumpet!

INTERESTS AND ACTIVITIES

(This item comes later in forms for applicants with longer employment histories)

Full answers in full sentences show the kind of person you are; how you participate – performing or contributing or passively; what you get from it; what you give back. Omit interests you have dropped.

WORK EXPERIENCE or EMPLOYMENT HISTORY

List employers in reverse date order with dates, position held, main duties and responsibilities, level of authority (if space allows). This also applies if your sole experience is vacation work, year-off activities, Saturday or early morning jobs. Mention voluntary work.

DESCRIBE:

Activities you have planned and organised. Team activities in which you have participated, and your role. Your greatest achievements.

These questions are likely to be directed to first-job applicants to large organisations. Think them through carefully and come up with something convincing. They want to find out the sort of person you are.

WHY HAVE YOU APPLIED TO THIS ORGANISATION?

WHAT CAN YOU OFFER?

WHAT CAREER PROGRESSION DO YOU HOPE FOR?

WHAT DO YOU EXPECT TO BE DOING IN FIVE YEARS' TIME?

10

HOW TO HANDLE THE RESULT

Have you been invited to come for interview? Excellent. If time allows, confirm the arrangements in writing (another neat letter): time, place and how to get there. Take along the copy of your CV, application form or letter.

Advertised vacancies

You may hear nothing, in which case, phone after a week or ten days to check that your application was received; use the opportunity to ask if anything else is likely to come up. But silence generally means you have not been short-listed, and you may have a letter later on when an appointment has been made. This highlights the fact that time can be lost waiting for responses.

Especially if you are unemployed, you need to make lots of applications to maintain morale and prevent a feeling of hopelessness creeping in. If you really are getting nowhere, ask friends or family to look through your copy applications and comment frankly on what they see. A fresh eye on the subject could pinpoint a flaw you have not noticed. Have you sought help from a Job Club? Do you need to acquire new skills or update existing ones?

A new job gives you the chance to reinvent yourself and present a new image to the world. Enjoy the experience.